PLANTS FOR
SUNNY
WINDOWS

Kenneth A. Beckett

Salem House

First published in the United States by
Salem House Publishers, 1989, 462 Boston Street,
Topsfield, Massachusetts, 01983.

Conceived and produced by
Swallow Books, 260 Pentonville Road,
London N1 9JY

ISBN: 0 88162 384 9
Art Director: Elaine Partington
Editor: Catherine Tilley
Designers: Jean Hoyes and Hilary Krag
Studio: Del & Co
Typesetters: Bournetype, Bournemouth
Printed in Italy by Imago Publishing Limited

Author's acknowledgments
The great majority of pictures in this book are of plants
growing in botanical and private gardens. My wife Gillian,
who took most of the colour transparencies, and I are
particularly grateful to the following people for their
cooperation in allowing us access to their plant
collections behind the scenes: Mr C. D. Brickell, formerly
Director of the RHS Gardens, Wisley, Dr R. D. Shaw,
Curator of the Royal Botanic Garden, Edinburgh and
Mr J. B. E. Simmons, Curator of the Royal Botanic
Gardens, Kew. We are especially indebted to
Mr L. Maurice Mason for allowing us unlimited time
among his treasures at Talbot Manor, Fincham, Norfolk
over the years. As a result, more of his plants feature in
this book than anyone else's.

INTRODUCTION

Traditionally, the place for plants in the home has been on the windowsill or on a table close to a window. Although today plants tend to be used more adventurously – often in the same way as ornaments and pictures – the windowsill is still the favourite position and, undoubtedly, the best place in terms of light and visibility. In the average home windows are now much larger than was once usual, providing more scope for growing plants. Bright light is essential for the healthy growth of many well-known houseplants, for example, pot geraniums (*Pelargonium*) and *Hibiscus* and a whole host of cacti and other succulents. There are numerous striking and often colourful plants which are good home dwellers if they get at least half a day of full sun when actively growing. All the plants described in this book come into this category, although a few might appreciate a little temporary shade during the hottest spells.

Light intensity and direction change with the passing year. In winter, when the sun arcs low in the south, only a south-facing window gets the full benefit of available light. All plants that grow in winter – notably bulbous subjects, including the hardy narcissus, tulips and hyacinths which provide so much winter colour in the home – should be placed in a south window. As the season advances and the sun climbs higher, the direct light leaves the south windows and shines longest into those facing east and west in the morning and afternoon. Windows facing due north may or may not receive a little direct sunlight in the early morning and late afternoon during the summer only. For the rest of the year they are totally sunless and not suitable for the plants described in this book.

Siting, choosing and buying

Sunlight is not the only factor to consider when choosing a plant. A light-demanding plant which also requires warm conditions will not thrive in a cool or unheated room. Basic information on warmth and watering requirements of the plants described here are given in at-a-glance easy-to-understand symbols.

The quality of houseplants offered for sale is, largely, very good. However, it is sensible to choose only the best specimens and to shop around if need be. Do not buy plants that look pale or have limp, flecked or crippled leaves. If the plant has flowers and buds, make sure they do not fall readily if you shake it gently. In winter, get the plant home as soon as possible, for prolonged chilling can result in partial or total falling or withering of leaves and flower buds.

Watering

Applying too much or too little water to a plant in a container is a primary cause of root failure and death. For the beginner, knowing when to water a plant can be a problem. Aim to keep the soil moist, but not wet. Too much water will result in a sour, constantly wet, soil ideal for root rot diseases. Too little can produce a slow-growing plant with small leaves and flowers that are very prone to wilt or being prematurely shed. The easiest way to decide when a plant needs water is to probe into the soil surface with your fingertip to a depth of about 1cm (½in). If the soil seems dry or barely damp, give the plant a good watering. This means filling up the gap between the soil surface and the pot rim. If the plant is a cactus or succulent, then all the soil must be allowed to get dry between waterings and little or no water is required between mid-autumn and mid-spring. Orchids must be watered in the same way but without the winter drought.

Humidity

Many of the plants described here come from areas of high rainfall where the air is humid, at least during the growing season. Although many of these plants are remarkably tolerant of the dry air in our homes, they will be, and look, healthier in moister air. This applies particularly to ferns and orchids, and even cacti and succulents when they are growing. There are three basic ways to provide sufficient humidity. The first is by plunging the pots into deep trays of moist peat. Alternatively, shallow trays of flooded gravel can be used, but make sure that the water surface is just below the top of the stones on which the containers stand. The third method is to use a fine droplet (mist) sprayer to wet the leaves at least once a day, except when temperatures drop below the average minimum.

Feeding

Sooner or later the nutrients in potting soil run out and plant growth slows to a standstill; at the same time, the lower leaves fall and all the young ones mature markedly smaller than usual, often being pale red or purple-tinged. Before this state is reached you must feed the plant. This is easy to do – simply apply one of the formulated liquid feeds available in garden centres, mixed according to makers' instructions. For a quick tonic, the so-called foliar feeds, containing highly soluble fertilizers plus a wetting agent, are useful.

Top-dressing

Long-term pot plants should be top-dressed annually in spring. With a small hand fork or a large kitchen fork strip away the top layer of soil and fine roots, removing about one-sixth to one-quarter of the total depth of the root ball. Do not damage the larger roots. Replace the discarded layer with fresh soil, which ideally should contain one of the granular, slow-release general fertilizers, then firm and water.

Pruning

Perennials, shrubs and climbers often grow too large and need cutting back from time to time. Climbers and shrubs are best thinned out when dormant or after flowering to let in light and air. This can be done by cutting out whole stems or branches to their bases or to ground level. The remaining growth can be shortened by one-quarter to one-third. Evergreen perennials such as *Zebrina* can be dealt with in much the same way, except that the remaining stems can be cut back by one-half or more. Deciduous or semi-deciduous perennials, for example, *Gloriosa, Lachenalia, Lapeirousia*, should be cut back to ground level as the foliage yellows.

How to use this book

This book contains a selection of the most suitable and readily available plants for sunny windows, together with descriptions of the plants in their mature state, and their requirements (temperature, watering, and so on). These are given in symbols, which are explained below. From this, you should be able to select a plant which meets your requirements exactly, and which will thrive in your home or conservatory. Although, as far as possible, technical terms have not been used in the main text of the book, there have been occasions when it has been impossible to avoid them. They are all explained in full in the glossary on page 63.

Symbol key

Cultural requirements and overall plant shape/growth habit are summarized in the form of at-a-glance symbols beside each entry. These provide quick reference and supplement the main description of the plant.

Temperature requirements

🌡 Tropical/warm – minimum 15–18°C (60–65°F)

🌡 Temperate – minimum 10–15°C (50–60°F)

🌡 Cool – minimum 5–10°C (40–50°F); down to −3°C (27°F) if noted as hardy

Watering requirements

🪣 Light – Allow rooting medium to dry out completely between waterings.

🪣 Medium – Allow surface of rooting medium to dry out between waterings.

🪣 Heavy – Keep entire rooting medium moist at all times.

Plant habit/shape

Ψ Erect

⇌ Spreading/prostrate

— Mat-forming

♀ Bushy

⋔ Weeping

⚐ Climbing/Scrambling

⌣ Rosette-forming

⋔ Pendent/Trailing

▼ Tufted/Fan-like/ Clump-forming

Ω Globular (or cylindrical)

ABUTILON

Malvaceae
Flowering maples

Origin: *Tropical to warm temperate areas of the world, especially South America, where they grow in light woodland and scrub. A genus of 100 evergreen shrubs, annuals and perennials which are grown for their hanging, bell-shaped flowers and long-stalked, maple-like leaves. All flower well when small, either grown on year after year or propagated annually from stem cuttings in spring or late summer. Abutilon derives from the Arabic name for mallow.*

Abutilon × *milleri*

Species cultivated

A. megapotamicum Brazil
Slender-stemmed shrub which grows to 2m (6½ft), the flowers having a crimson calyx and yellow petals. Suitable for temperate conditions. *A.m.* 'Variegatum' has yellow blotched leaves.

A. × milleri
A hybrid of *A. megapotamicum* and very similar to that species, but more robust with red-veined, yellow flowers. 'Kentish Belle' *(A. megapotamicum* × 'Golden Fleece') has orange-red petals and a grey-red calyx. Suitable for temperate conditions.

AEONIUM

Crassulaceae

Origin: *Arabia, Ethiopia, the Mediterranean region and the North Atlantic islands. A genus of 40 species of succulents, many of which thrive in the home, and are very decorative when in bloom. They have fleshy, elongated leaves in rosettes – some species form a single rosette,*

Aeonium simsii

others produce several. Many species are shrubby, their rosettes standing on a woody stem. The starry flowers have six to 12 petals and occur in rounded or pyramid-shaped panicles at the ends of the stems. Stems die after flowering and are best cut out (solitary species die completely after flowering). Propagate by seed or by leaf or stem cuttings in spring or summer. Aeonium *is the Latin name for what is now* A. arboreum.

Species cultivated

A. arboreum Portugal, Spain, Morocco, Sicily and Sardinia
Sparsely branched shrub which grows to 1m (3ft) in height. Leaves are glossy, bright green, fleshy and 5–9cm (2–3½in) long. Panicles of bright yellow flowers open at the ends of the branches from winter to spring. *A. a.* 'Atropurpureum' is similar, but with very striking dark, glossy-purple leaves.

A. simsii (*A. caespitosum*) Gran Canaria
Tufted perennial, forming cushions of more or less stalkless rosettes. The very narrow and lance-shaped leaves are 3–6cm (1¼–2½in) long, green in colour and with prominent soft white hairs at the edges. Golden-yellow flowers occur freely in spring, making this a most attractive species.

AGAVE

Agavaceae
Century plants

Origin: *Southern North America to northern South America. A genus of 300 species of succulent evergreen perennials, grown indoors mainly for their leaves – young specimens make good houseplants while larger ones make imposing plants for the conservatory. They form stemless rosettes of thick, fleshy, usually spine-tipped leaves (beware of their sharpness). Flowers do not develop on specimens grown in containers unless they are grown in very large tubs; nor do leaves reach full size where the roots are restricted. When they do appear, the flowers are numerous, greenish or brownish and small, but carried in towering racemes or candelabra-like clusters at the tops of long stems. Once it has flowered the rosette always dies, but is replaced by offsets or stem bulbils from which new plants can be propagated. Seed, when available, should be sown in spring.* Agave *derives from the Greek* agavos, *admirable, from the appearance of a plant in full bloom, which is worthy of admiration.*

Species cultivated

A. americana Century plant, Maguey, American aloe Mexico, Naturalized elsewhere
Leaves are grey-green, and grow to 1.5m (5ft) and up to 20cm (8in) in

Agave americana medio-picta

width. In warm climates flowering stems can reach 8m (26ft). Fermented sap from the cut flowering stem gives the Mexican national drink, pulque. There are several variegated forms.

A.a. marginata

Leaves have two pale yellow bands on the edges.

A.a. marginata-alba

Leaves have two white to cream bands on the edges and are suffused with pink when young.

Agave victoriae-reginae

A.a. medio-picta

Leaves have a central yellow stripe.

A. filifera Thread agave Mexico

Numerous very narrow to lance-shaped leaves, edged with whitish, horny threads. Flowers form a dense cylindrical raceme which grows to 2.5m (8ft) tall. This is a good pot plant because of its lack of spines.

A. victoriae-reginae Mexico

Shapely rosettes rather resembling a globe artichoke, with 15cm (6in) long, broad, dark green, blunt leaves with white lines and horny edges, ending abruptly in a short spine. The flowering spike can reach 4m (13ft).

ALOE
Liliaceae

Origin: *Africa, particularly south of the equator, Malagasy and Arabia, where they grow in arid and semi-desert areas often among or beneath sparse scrub. A genus of 275 species of evergreen leaf succulents grown both for their ornamental leaves and red, yellow or orange flowers. The largest species are erect and tree-like, the smallest are perennial and grow in clumps or mounds. In between are shrubby species of varying size and vigour and a group of semi-climbers or sprawlers with greatly elongated stems and well-spaced leaves. Apart from the latter, the generally lance-shaped, sometimes mottled or patterned fleshy leaves are carried in tufts or rosettes. The tubular flowers, composed of six narrow tepals, are arranged in simple or branched racemes well above the leaves. They are often very showy and open mainly in late spring and summer.* Aloe *derives from the Arabic name* Alloeh.

Species cultivated

A. arborescens South Africa
Erect plant which grows to 1–4m (3–13ft) tall with leaves reaching 60cm (2ft) long, usually grey-green. Flowers are red, 4–4.5cm (1½–1¾in) long, in simple racemes borne in winter. *A.a.* 'Variegata' has attractive creamy white striped foliage.

A. ciliaris Climbing aloe South Africa
Stem is flexible, branched, scrambling or prostrate, growing to 5m (16ft) or more. Very narrow, lance-shaped leaves up to 15cm (6in). Flowers are 3cm (1¼in) long, scarlet, yellow-green tipped, in usually simple racemes.

Below left *Aloe ciliaris*
Below *Aloe arborescens*
'Variegata'

A. variegata South Africa
Clump-forming, eventually having a 15cm (6in) stem. Leaves are 11cm (4½in) long, triangular to spear-shaped, keeled and closely overlapping, dark green, strongly cross-banded with white spots. Flowers are tubular, salmon-red, and in loose racemes.

ANIGOZANTHOS
Haemodoraceae

Origin: *Western Australia. A genus of ten strikingly unusual species of evergreen, clump-forming to tufted perennials with narrow, sword-shaped leaves. The woolly, long-tubular flowers are split at the mouth beneath and open out into six claw-like segments, supposedly resembling a kangaroo's paw; they are borne in undivided or, more usually, branched racemes well above the foliage. Propagate by seed in spring, or by division after flowering or in spring. Anigozanthos derives from the Greek anoigo, to open and anthos, a flower, alluding to the way the tubular blooms are split on one side.*

Species cultivated
A. manglesii Common green/Mangle's kangaroo paw
Clump-forming species whose stems grow to 90cm (3ft) tall. Flowers are 8cm (3in) long, bright red at the base, the rest vivid green, borne on red stems in branched racemes in spring and summer. The best-known species and the floral emblem of Western Australia.

Anigozanthos manglesii

Asclepias curassavica

ASCLEPIAS
Asclepiadaceae

Origin: *North and South America. A genus of 120 species of perennials and sub-shrubs some of which are tuberous-rooted. They have opposite pairs or whorls of lance-shaped to oval leaves and five-petalled flowers in umbels. Each flower has five stamens, which are joined in a tube within which the anthers are attached to the stigma. The fruits are pod-like follicles which contain seeds crowned by long silky hairs for wind dispersal. Many species exude a poisonous milky latex when cut or damaged. Propagate by seed in spring.* Asclepias *derives from the name of the Greek god of medicine,* Asklepios, *in a Latinized form.*

Species cultivated
A. curassavica Blood flower Tropical America
Sub-shrub growing to 90cm (3ft) or so in height. Lance-shaped leaves are carried in pairs 5–15cm (2–6in) long. Flowers reach to 2cm (¾in) wide, orange-red with a yellow tube crown; they are borne in umbels of five to ten, opening in summer and autumn. A good long-term houseplant, even better in the conservatory.

ASTROPHYTUM
Cactaceae

Origin: *Mexico. A genus of six species of globular to short cylindrical cacti of distinctive form, some having prominent ribs, variously studded with scale-like branched, white hairs. The areoles are small and woolly, the upper ones bearing the funnel-shaped flowers. Propagate by seed. All species are successful houseplants.* Astrophytum *derives from the Greek* astron, *a star and* phyton, *plant, referring to their more or less star shape when seen from above.*

Astrophytum ornatum

Species cultivated

A. ornatum

Short cylindrical stem, which with age reaches 30cm (1ft) in height and 12–15cm (4¾–6in) in diameter. Eight sharp and deep ribs bear along their edges, areoles with five to 11 awl-shaped and amber to brown spines 3–4cm (1¼–1½in) long. Flowers, which are 7–9cm (2¾–3½in) wide and a clear yellow colour, do not occur on young plants.

BOUGAINVILLEA

Nyctaginaceae

Origin: *Tropical and sub-tropical areas of South America. A genus of 18 species of shrubs and scrambling climbers. Those described here are climbers having alternate, oval to elliptic leaves and groups of*

Bougainvillea glabra

three small flowers, each made up of three tubular tepals, the whole surrounded by three large, colourful, papery bracts. These in turn are arranged in panicle-like clusters, of which there are many. They are very colourful climbers suitable for large pots or tubs in the conservatory, where they can be trained on to a wall or under the roof. They will also flower when young in small pots in the home. Bougainvillea *was named for Louis Antoine de Bougainville (1729– 1811), a French navigator and sailor who circumnavigated the world in 1767–9.*

Species cultivated

B. × buttiana

A hybrid between *B. glabra* and *B. peruviana* reaching 6m (20ft) or more in height. Leaves are very variable in form, broadly oval, sometimes growing to 18cm (7in) long on vigorous stems, usually less than this. The flowers grow in clusters at the sides or ends of the stems. Many cultivars are available.

B. glabra Paper flower Brazil

Grows to 4m (13ft) or more. Leaves are elliptic, growing to about 8cm (3in) long. Bracts grow to 4cm (1½in) long in shades of cyclamen-purple. Several cultivars are grown including: 'Cypheri', strong-growing, with leaves to 11cm (4½in) and bracts to 6cm (2½in); 'Sanderiana', especially good for pot culture, flowers freely when small; and 'Variegata', with leaves which are boldly variegated with white. A useful foliage plant.

Campanula isophylla 'Alba'

CAMPANULA
Campanulaceae

Origin: *Northern temperate latitudes and into sub-tropical and tropical zones as a mountain plant. A genus of 300 species of annuals, perennials and sub-shrubs, the majority of which are herbaceous perennials. All have five-lobed flowers which vary from the typical tubular bell shape to wide open stars.* C. isophylla *makes a charming basket plant for the conservatory or cool room. Propagate by seed in spring or by division.* Campanula *is a diminutive form of the Latin* campana, *a bell.*

Species cultivated
C. isophylla Italian bellflower N.W. Italy
A tufted species, with trailing stems reaching 20cm (8in) or more. Leaves are rounded and heart-shaped, toothed, the ones at the base of the stem soon falling, and less than half the length of the stem leaves. Flowers are widely funnel-shaped, almost starry, 1.5–2.5cm (½–1in) across, lilac-blue in colour and borne in late summer. *C.i.* 'Alba' has white flowers; 'Mayi' is a softly hairy plant; 'Variegata' has white-variegated leaves.

CANARINA
Campanulaceae

Origin: *Canary Isles and East Africa. A genus of three species of tuberous-rooted perennials with scrambling stems and large hanging bell-flowers. They are allied to* Campanula *but are distinct in having leaves in pairs and fleshy fruits. The species described here is not only beautiful, but flowers in winter and is an especially valuable*

easy-to-cultivate plant. Canarina *derives from the Canary Isles, homeland of the first described species.*

Species cultivated

C. canariensis (*C. campanula*)
Stems cluster at ground level, are 2–3m (6½–10ft) long and need support. Leaves are narrowly triangular, irregularly toothed, 5–8cm (2–3in) long, and slightly blue-green above, more so beneath. Flowers are widely bell-shaped, about 6cm (2½in) long, and pale orange with darker veins. They hang at the tips of lateral branchlets and appear in late autumn to early spring.

Canarina canariensis

CATHARANTHUS
Apocynaceae

Origin: *Tropical and sub-tropical Malagasy; one species from India. A genus of five species of evergreen sub-shrubs closely allied to* Vinca *(periwinkle), which it resembles. The species described below is the only one generally cultivated and has become widely naturalized throughout the tropics. It makes a charming pot plant. Propagate by seed or cuttings in spring.* Catharanthus *derives from the Greek* katharos, *clean or without blemish and* anthos, *a flower.*

Catharanthus roseus

Species cultivated

C. roseus (*Vinca rosea*) Madagascar periwinkle
An erect or spreading species growing to 60cm (2ft). Leaves are 3–10cm (1¼–4in) long, oblong to oval, glossy green. Rose-pink to white flowers have a slender tube up to 2.5cm (1in) long, which open to five flat, petal-like lobes to about 4cm (1½in) across in spring and summer. *C.r. ocellatus* has white flowers with a red or pink eye; dwarf strains to 20cm (8in) high are available and are excellent for pots.

CEROPEGIA
Asclepediaceae

Origin: *Tropical and sub-tropical Africa, Asia, Malagasy, Canary Isles and Australia. A genus of 160 species of shrubby or twining perennials, some with fleshy or tuberous roots. The sometimes succulent stems bear opposite pairs of rounded to very narrow leaves which in some species soon fall. The remarkable flowers are tubular, often inflated at the base; their five corolla lobes can be bent back or joined at the tips to form a cage or, in some species where the tips of the lobes are expanded and membraneous, an umbrella-like shape. They grow well in the home or conservatory, making intriguing pot or basket plants. Propagate by seed in spring or by cuttings in spring*

Above *Ceropegia woodii*
Right *Ceropegia fusca*

or summer in warmth. Ceropegia *derives from* keros, *wax and* pege, *a fountain, the flowers of some species are said to resemble a fountain formed from wax.*

Species cultivated

C. fusca Canary Isles (Tenerife, Gran Canaria)
Stems are grey-white, growing to 90cm (3ft) tall. Flowers are dark brownish-red.

C. woodii String of hearts, Rosary vine Natal, South Africa
Slender creeping or hanging stems, which grow to 60cm (2ft) or more, often with small, aerial tubers at the nodes. Leaves are heart-shaped, fleshy, purple, the upper sides strongly marbled with silver and 1.5–2cm (⅝–¾in) long. Flowers are red to reddish-brown, about 2cm (¾in) long, slightly curved, inflated at the base and expanded at the mouth, and have narrow lobes.

CHAMAECEREUS

Cactaceae

Origin: *Argentina. A genus of only one species of cactus which has been classified as a* Cereus, *and by some botanists is now included in* Lobivia *It is a very easy plant to grow and will thrive with the*

Chamaecereus silvestrii

minimum of attention. Propagate by detaching stem segments, which root readily. Chamaecereus *derives from the Greek* chamai, *dwarf and* Cereus, *a genus of cacti.*

Species cultivated

C. silvestrii Peanut cactus
A small prostrate cactus eventually forming mats to 30cm (1ft) across. Stems are cylindrical, branched into short, oblong to egg-shaped (or peanut-shaped) segments and grow to 6cm (2½in) long and 1.5cm (⅝in) wide. They have eight to ten shallow ribs with numerous small, white areoles bearing tiny, bristle-like spines. Flowers are orange-scarlet, funnel-shaped, 5–7cm (2–2¾in) long, and open from early spring. Hybrids between this species and members of the genus *Lobivia* are sometimes grown.

CHRYSANTHEMUM

Compositae

Origin: *Northern temperate zone. A genus of 200 species of annuals, perennials and shrubs, several of which are mainstay plants in the garden, greenhouse and conservatory. The species described below is typified by showy daisy flowers usually freely borne over a long period. Its colour embellishes the conservatory and it can be brought into the home when in bloom. Propagate by seed or cuttings in spring; also by cuttings in late summer or early autumn.* Chrysanthemum *derives from the Greek* chrysos, *gold and* anthos, *a flower.*

Species cultivated

C. frutescens (*Argyranthemum frutescens*) Marguerite Canary Isles
Frost-tender shrub of rounded habit, reaching 30–60cm (1–2ft) in

Chrysanthemum frutescens 'Jamaica Primrose'

height. Leaves are evergreen, usually with lobes which are again lobed, 4–8cm (1½–3in) long, sometimes more or less blue-green. The 2cm (¾in) wide, white flowers have yellow discs and white rays and occur intermittently all the year. Most of the plants grown as *C. frutescens* are, however, hybrids with other Canary Isles species, e.g. *C. coronopifolium*; popularly known as Paris daisies, they have flower heads 5–8cm (2–3in) wide, some with yellow or pink ray florets, singles and doubles. All are extremely useful conservatory and sunny home window plants since they will flower in winter, provided a minimum day temperature of 13°C (55°F) can be maintained.

CLEISTOCACTUS

Cactaceae

Origin: *South America. A genus of 30 species of cacti with slender erect or decumbent, columnar stems having many ribs bearing small, closely set round areoles. The flowers are narrow, tubular and curved*

to almost straight. Fruits are small, globular berries. They grow well in the home or conservatory, flowering freely. Propagate by seed in spring or by cuttings of stem tips in summer. Cleistocactus *derives from the Greek* kleistos, *closed, the flowers barely open.*

Species cultivated

C. baumannii (*Cereus baumannii*) Scarlet bugler Argentina, Uruguay, Paraguay
Stems grow to 1m (3ft) or more tall, with about 14 ribs bearing yellow-brown areoles; each has 15 to 20 4cm (1½in) long spines. Flowers are orange-scarlet, asymmetric, 6–7cm (2½–2¾in) long, opening in summer and followed by red 1.2cm (½in) fruits.

C. strausii (*Cereus strausii, Borzicactus strausii, Pilocereus strausii*) Bolivia
Stems grow to 1m (3ft) or more in length, branch from the base and have about 25 ribs; the closely set areoles have 30 hair-like white bristles and three to four pale yellow or white spines, giving a white-woolly effect. Flowers are 8–9cm (3–3½in) long and red.

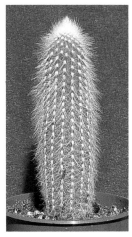

Cleistocactus strausii

CORYPHANTHA
Cactaceae

Origin: North America to Cuba. A genus of 64 species of cacti, formerly classified under Mammillaria *and by some botanists considered to include only 20 to 30 species. They have rounded to cylindrical stems, 2.5–15cm (1–6in) long. The tubercles are prominent, each with a marked groove along the upper side and tipped with a spine-bearing areole. The flowers are comparatively large and widely funnel-shaped. They grow well in a conservatory or the home, and need a cool rest in winter. Propagate by seed in spring or by offsets, if available, in summer.* Coryphantha *derives from the Greek* korypha, *summit and* anthos, *a flower, the flowers being borne at the top of the plant body.*

Coryphantha bumamma

Species cultivated
C. bumamma Mexico

Single globe-shaped stem reaching 12cm (4¾in) in time. Tubercles are rounded, flattened above, the groove woolly. Six to eight radial spines, though no central spines. Flowers are yellow to reddish, 8–10cm (3–4in) wide. Considered by some botanists to be a form of the closely allied *C. elephantidens* which has red to pink flowers.

CYPERUS
Cyperaceae

Origin: *Tropical, sub-tropical and warm temperate regions throughout the world. A genus of 550 species of evergreen perennials with a few annuals. Those cultivated are all perennials, a few grow from tubers, but most from rhizomes or stolons. They have tapering grass-like leaves and tiny, petalless flowers each made up of a single ovary and one to three stamens enclosed in bractlets and arranged in flattened, grass-like spikelets. These make up umbels or heads of flowers. All may be grown in pots in a conservatory and the smaller species are good in the home, especially in cool rooms. Propagate by division or seed in spring.*

Cyperus alternifolius

Cyperus *is the Greek word for a sedge.*

Species cultivated
C. alternifolius Umbrella grass/plant Malagasy, Mauritius

Clump-forming with stiff or channelled stems reaching 60–120cm (2–4ft) tall. Leaves are slender, 20–40cm (4–8in) long and borne around the top of the stem like the spokes of an umbrella. Green to brown flowers are borne in stalked spikelets at the centre of the leaf rosette. In the wild it is a bog plant, in a pot it is best if stood in a saucer or tray of water. *C.a.* 'Gracilis' is much smaller, only 30–45cm (12–18in) tall. *C.a.* 'Variegatus' has leaves which are striped longitudinally with white, sometimes all white.

ECHEVERIA
Crassulaceae

Origin: *The Americas from S.W. USA to Mexico and Argentina. A genus of 150 species of decorative evergreen succulent perennials which are usually stemless with rosettes of fleshy, often attractive leaves. The flowers are tubular to bell-shaped with five fleshy petals. Propagate by detaching rosettes or by leaf cuttings, both in summer, or by division or seed in spring.* Echeveria *was named for the Spanish botanical artist Athanasio Echeverria Godoy, who accompanied an expedition to Mexico in 1787–97.*

Species cultivated

Echeveria glauca

E. glauca (*E. secunda glauca*) Blue echeveria
Clump-forming, usually stemless with rosettes up to 10cm (4in) across. Leaves are 2.5–8cm (1–3in) long, broadly oval, and very blue-green with a blue-grey patina and sometimes with a narrow reddish edge. Flowers are 8–10cm (⅓–⅜in) long, bright red, and occur in racemes 20–30cm (8–12in) tall, which are erect at first, then arch at the tips, and open in spring and summer.

E. harmsii (*Oliveranthus elegans*)
Branched sub-shrub, with stems eventually reaching 30cm (1ft) tall. Leaves are 2–3cm (¾–1¼in) long and clustered at the stem tips, but not in a true rosette; they are lance- or spatula-shaped, keeled beneath and green. Flowers are 2–3cm (¾–1¼in) long, narrowly urn-shaped and scarlet, and the petals tipped with yellow; they are borne singly or in twos or threes on stalks 10–20cm (4–8in) long in late spring and summer.

Echinocereus reichenbachii perbellus

ECHINOCEREUS
Cactaceae

Origin: *Southern North America. A genus of 75 species of cactus, generally clump-forming with oval to cylindrical stems usually less than 40cm (16in) long, either erect, sprawling or hanging. Most have very spiny areoles and widely funnel-shaped showy flowers in summer. Their fruits are spiny. Propagate by seed or by cuttings in summer.* Echinocereus *derives from the Greek* echinos, *a hedgehog and* cereus, *a closely allied cactus genus with spineless fruits.*

Species cultivated

E. caespitosus See *E. reichenbachii.*

E. reichenbachii (*E. caespitosus*) Lace cactus USA (Texas), Mexico Usually single-stemmed, spherical at first, later cylindrical, erect, growing up to 20cm (8in) high. Ten to 19 ribs with closely set areoles. There are 12 to 36 comb-like radial spines of varying lengths, white or yellowish with darker tips, and also one or two (rarely as many as seven) central ones, although these are often absent. Flowers are 6–7cm (2½–2¾in) long and bright pink.

E.r. perbellus
Stems branch from the base, are 5–10cm (2–4in) high with closely set areoles. Twelve to 15 radial spines, about 1.5cm (⅝in) long, brownish or reddish. Purple flowers are 4–6cm (1½–2½in) long.

ECHINOFOSSULOCACTUS
Cactaceae

Origin: *Mexico. A genus of 32 species of variable cacti, included by some botanists in the genus* Stenocactus. *Most are globular or short and cylindrical with attractive spines and often showy blooms. Most*

*Echinofossulocactus
zacatecasensis*

*species are free-flowering. Propagate by seed in spring in warmth.
Echinofossulocactus derives from the Greek echinos, a hedgehog, the
Latin fossulo, a ditch and cactus, the hollows between the spiny ribs
being very marked.*

Species cultivated

E. zacatecasensis Brain cactus
Found near Zacatecas, Mexico, hence the tongue-twisting name.
Globe-shaped, pale green, growing to 10cm (4in) in diameter, and
having about 55 thin, wavy ribs, with the upper areoles white-woolly.
Ten to 12 white radial spines, slender and spreading, to 1cm (⅜in)
long, three central ones, the middle one thick, flattened and straight
to 4cm (1½in) long, the outer two shorter and hooked. Flowers are
3–4cm (1¼–1½in) across, with white petals tipped with pink.

ECHINOPSIS
Cactaceae
Sea urchin cacti

*Origin: South America. A genus of 35 species of globular or
cylindrical cacti with prominently ribbed, solitary or clump-forming
stems and trumpet-shaped flowers often with very long tubes. They are
very tolerant house or conservatory plants. Propagate by offsets or by
seed. Echinopsis derives from the Greek echinus, a hedgehog and
opsis, like.*

Species cultivated

E. eyriesii (*Echinocactus eyriesii*) Argentina, southern Brazil
With a globe-shaped stem branching from the base, becoming

Echinopsis werdermanniana

elongated with age, growing to about 15cm (6in) in diameter. There are 11 to 18 ribs with round, well-spaced woolly areoles, ten radial spines and four to eight central ones, all dark brown. Flowers are 22cm (10in) long from base of tube, pure white and open widely to 12cm (4¾in) across.

E. werdermanniana (*Trichocereus werdermanniana*) Bolivia

The cylindrical stems grow eventually to the size of a tree, are green to grey, and reach 60cm (2ft) in diameter at the base. In its young state, however, this species is very decorative, with six ribs (later up to 12), bearing white, closely set areoles. Twelve to 18 radial spines which grow to 4cm (1½in) long, are fawny-yellow becoming grey; six to nine central spines are reddish-brown becoming horny. Flowers open at the top and are pink when young, becoming more red with age.

ERICA

Ericaceae
Heaths

Origin: *Chiefly South Africa, but some from North Atlantic islands, Europe and North Africa to Turkey and Syria. A genus of about 600 species of wiry-stemmed evergreen shrubs with very narrow to oblong leaves, usually with rolled-under edges. The flowers are bell- or urn-shaped and very freely borne. Most ericas need an acid, peaty compost as they live in association with a fungus that lives within the entire plant, but particularly in the roots (endotrophic mycorrhiza), and helps to provide essential minerals. These fungi mostly require acid conditions. Those species described below are best in the conservatory, but can be brought into the home for flowering.*

Propagate by cuttings in spring (E. carnea in late summer); species also by seed in spring.

Erica *derives from the Greek* ereike *or the Latin* erice, *ancient names for the tree heath,* Erica arborea, *which is common in the Mediterranean region.*

Species cultivated

E. cerinthoides South Africa
Erect and bushy, growing to 60–90cm (2–3ft) tall. Leaves are very narrow and 1.2cm (½in) long, in whorls of four to six. Crimson flowers occur in clusters at the ends of the stems, and are 2–3cm (¾–1¼in) long, tubular, slightly inflated in the middle and constricted at the mouth. They appear from early summer until autumn. Temperate.

Erica cerinthoides

E. × hyemalis South African hybrid
Erect shrub which grows to 60cm (2ft) with 5–10mm (⅕–⅜in) very narrow leaves. Flowers are 1.5–2cm (⅝–¾in) long, tubular, rose-pink shading to white at the mouth. They are carried in long racemes in autumn and winter. Temperate.

E. versicolor South Africa
Freely branching, more or less erect, reaching 60–120cm (2–4ft) in height. Very narrow leaves are 4mm (⅙in) long, and occur in whorls of three. Flowers, which occur in clusters of three and top all the short lateral stems, are 2–2.5cm (¾–1in) long.

EUCOMIS

Liliaceae
Pineapple lilies

Origin: *Tropical and southern Africa. A genus of 14 species of bulbous perennials, whose bulbs have widened, almost stem-like base plates and fleshy-textured strap-shaped leaves. Their flowers are six-tepalled, star-shaped and usually in shades of green or white. They are carried in cylindrical racemes and topped by a tuft of green leaves. They are best in the cool conservatory but can be tried in the home, and are best repotted annually in early spring. Propagate by removing offsets, or by seed, both in spring.* Eucomis *derives from the Greek* eu, *good and* kome, *hair, the tufts at the ends of the leaf-like bracts supposedly resembling a good head of hair.*

Eucomis autumnalis

Species cultivated

E. autumnalis (*E. undulata*) South Africa
Broadly lance-shaped leaves growing to 60cm (2ft) long, with wavy edges and grooved at the mid-vein. Flowers are 1–1.5cm (⅜–⅝in) wide, greenish or white in 45cm (1½ft) long cylindrical racemes, from late summer to autumn.

EUPHORBIA
Euphorbiaceae

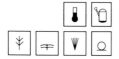

Below Euphorbia fulgens
Bottom Euphorbia pulcherrima

Origin: *Cosmopolitan, though most frequent in sub-tropics and warm temperate regions. A genus of some 2,000 species of annuals, perennials and shrubs, many of which are succulent. They differ vegetatively in almost every respect, but florally they are remarkably alike. All have a cyathium – a small cup-shaped whorl of bracts which are fused together. At the base of the cyathia are separate pairs of bracts called raylet leaves, and a ring of larger bracts called pseudumbel leaves at the base of each pseudumbel. These can be brightly coloured, as in poinsettia. The fruits, which are three-lobed capsules, open explosively. The species described here are suitable for the conservatory and home, especially when small. Succulents need a dry resting season. Both* E. fulgens *and* E. pulcherrima *are short-day plants needing 9–10 hours of darkness for about three months before the flowers start to bud. This can easily be carried out by covering with a box or blinds sufficiently early each evening to give the required amount of darkness. The milky latex of most species of* Euphorbia *is highly irritant to eyes, mouth and tender skin. Propagate by seed, division where possible or by cuttings in summer; for the succulent species washing the ends of the cuttings or dipping them in powdered charcoal and allowing them to dry for several days before insertion.* Euphorbia *was reputedly named for Euphorbos, doctor to the king of Mauritania.*

Species cultivated

E. fulgens Scarlet plume Mexico
Elegant deciduous shrub growing to 1.2m (4ft) tall. Stems are slender, arching, wand-like, usually sparingly branched. Leaves are elliptic to lance-shaped 5–10cm (2–4in) long, bright green. Cyathia with petal-like appendages, in small clusters from all the upper leaf axils, create bright scarlet sprays in winter.

E. pulcherrima Poinsettia Mexico
A familiar pot plant, usually seen below 1m (3ft) in height, but in the wild reaching to 4m (13ft). Leaves grow to 15cm (6in) or more long, oval to lance-shaped, toothed and sometimes lobed. Pseudumbel leaves, normally bright red, grow in clusters to 15–30cm (6–12in) across. Cultivars in shades of pink and white are also available.

EUSTOMA
Gentianaceae

Origin: *Mexico, southern USA, northern South America. A genus of three species of perennials, annuals or biennials, one of which is now*

making a comeback as a highly decorative flowering pot plant. It is best grown in the conservatory, but can be brought successfully into the home when in bloom. Propagate by division in autumn or by seed in early spring. Eustoma derives from the Greek eu, good and stoma, mouth, but is used in the most literal sense for a 'pretty face', e.g. the lovely flowers.

Eustoma grandiflorum

Species cultivated

E. grandiflorum (*E. russellianum, Lisianthus russellianus*) Prairie gentian Colorado and Nebraska to Texas and northern Mexico Erect perennial grown as an annual or biennial, 60–90cm (2–3ft) in height. Undivided leaves in opposite pairs, grow to 8cm (3in) long, oblong to oval. Flowers are five-petalled, opening widely bowl-shaped to 5cm (2in) in width, pale satiny purple in loose corymbose clusters in summer at the ends of the stems. The original species is not too easy to grow, but plant breeders have been working on it and there are new compact seed strains 35–45cm (14–18in) tall in shades of blue, pink, purple and white. Recommended are: 'Yodel Blue', 'Yodel Pink' and 'Yodel White'.

GERBERA
Compositae

Origin: *Africa, and Asia east to Bali. A genus of 70 species of herbaceous perennials with leaves in rosettes and single flowers on long stalks. The flowers of wild species have one or two rows of ray florets. They are attractive flowering plants for the sunny conservatory or home and are best re-propagated every two or three years to keep them compact. Gerberas are also very long-lasting as cut flowers. Propagate by seed, by division or by cuttings of non-flowering shoots,* *Gerbera* hybrid *all in spring. Gerbera was named for Traugott Gerber (d. 1743), a German naturalist and traveller.*

Species cultivated
G. jamesonii Barberton daisy South Africa
Clump-forming, with 25–40cm (10–16in) long, deeply pinnately lobed, oblong to spatula-shaped leaves, dull green above, white-woolly beneath. Flowers grow to 10cm (4in) wide, yellow to orange-red, on leafless stems to 45cm (1½ft) high.

Hybrids and seed strains
These come in a wide range of colours including red, pink, orange, yellow and white; many are double or semi-double.
'Happipot' is a dwarf seed strain 20–30cm (8–12in) high, bred especially for growing in pots. The flowers are semi-double to double and up to 8.5cm (3½in) across.

GLORIOSA
Liliaceae
Creeping/Climbing lilies

Origin: *Africa and Asia. A genus of five species of perennial climbers with narrow, rather brittle tubers. They bear slender stems and oblong to lance-shaped leaves often elongated at the tip into small tendrils. The long-stalked showy blooms are borne singly from the axils of the upper leaves and are normally red or yellow or a combination of the two. The six tepals bend backwards sharply and are sometimes waved;* *Gloriosa rothschildiana* *the six stamens spread widely beneath them. They are suitable for large pots in a conservatory and can be allowed to climb through a shrub or be supported by twiggy sticks, and if there is enough room they can be brought into the house for flowering. Pot the tubers in spring and dry off after they have flowered when the leaves begin to yellow; store dry through the winter. Propagate by separating offsets or by seed in spring.*
Gloriosa *is the Latin word for glorious.*

Species cultivated
G. rothschildiana Glory lily Tropical Africa
Grows to 2m (6½ft) tall. Leaves are broadly oval to lance-shaped, up to 18cm (7in) long and up to 5cm (2in) wide. Flowers are red with yellow edges, the yellow changing to red as it ages; tepals are strongly bent back and wavy edged, 5–8cm (2–3in) long.

GREVILLEA

Proteaceae

Origin: *Australia, New Caledonia to E. Malaysia. A genus of 190 species of evergreen trees and shrubs with alternate leaves, often pinnately divided, and racemes of petalless flowers, their bright colours coming from the calyx (or perianth) tube from which the long style protrudes.* G. robusta *is a large tree in the wild and is grown as a pot plant entirely for its leaves. Propagate by seed sown in spring or by cuttings taken with a heel in summer with bottom heat. Grevillea was named for Charles Francis Greville (1749–1809), a founder of the Horticultural Society of London.*

Species cultivated
G. robusta Silky oak Queensland, New South Wales (Australia)
A tree growing to 30m (100ft) in the wild, but in a pot rarely reaching over 2–3m (6½–10ft). Leaves are fern-like, bipinnately lobed, to 45cm (1½ft) long on young plants, smaller and less deeply cut when mature, rich green above, silky-hairy beneath. Flowers occur in one-sided racemes, and are golden-yellow, but appearing on mature trees only.

Grevillea robusta

Gymnocalycium baldianum

GYMNOCALYCIUM

Cactaceae

Origin: *South America. A genus of 60 species of globe-shaped to shortly cylindrical cacti with prominent ribs bearing areoles above 'chin-like' projections. They have relatively few spines, which are stout and usually curve backwards, and generally conspicuous, funnel- to trumpet-shaped flowers. They make good plants for the conservatory or home, needing a cool rest in winter. Propagate by seed in spring or by removing offsets in summer.* Gymnocalycium *derives from the Greek* gymnos, *naked and* kalyx, *a bud, the flower buds of this genus lacking spines, bristles or hair.*

Species cultivated

G. baldianum (*G. venturianum*) Argentina
Single stems, growing to 4.5cm (1¾in) high by 7cm (2¾in) wide, depressed at the top, dark grey-green, with small areoles on nine to 11 broadly rounded ribs. Five radial spines, about 6mm (¼in) long, yellowish to grey but no central spines. Flowers are about 4cm (1½in) long, funnel-shaped, red.

G. mihanovichii Paraguay
Globe-shaped stem, somewhat flattened, greyish-green, growing to 5cm (2in) wide. About eight ribs, broadly triangular, with small, closely set areoles. Seven to eight radial spines are yellowish to pale brown, 4cm (1½in) long; no central spines. Flowers are 4–5cm (1½–2in) long, yellow-green to reddish.

A number of mutant forms have arisen lacking chlorophyll, and yellow or red in colour. Being unable to produce their own food they can be maintained only by grafting on to a green stock, cuttings of a *Hylocereus* being frequently used. These mutants are widely available under such names as 'Red Head', 'Red Cap', 'Yellow Cap', 'Hibotan' (yellow) and 'Blondie'.

HABRANTHUS
Amaryllidaceae

Origin: *Sub-tropical and tropical America. A genus of perhaps 20 species of bulbous plants related to both* Hippeastrum *and* Zephyranthes *and in appearance much like a diminutive version of the former, but with only one flower per stem. Easily grown in pots, they make pleasing short-term flowering plants for home and conservatory. Propagate by seed, or offsets removed when re-potting, both in spring. Plants are best left in their containers until fairly congested before dividing. Keep dry during the winter.*

Habranthus *derives from the Greek* habros, *graceful and* anthos, *a flower.*

Species cultivated

H. tubispathus (*H. robustus, Zephyranthes robusta*) Argentina
The leaves are narrowly strap-shaped, spreading and curving backwards, about 22cm (9in) long, usually developing after blooming. The flowering stems grow up to 22cm (9in) or more in height, topped by a 6–8cm (2½–3in) wide flower; the tepals are rose-red or pink with a hint of purple, shading to white at the base and appearing in early autumn.

Habranthus tubispathus

HIBISCUS
Malvaceae

Origin: *Tropics and sub-tropics. A genus of 250 to 300 species of annuals, perennials, shrubs and trees with alternate lobed leaves, often shaped like the palm of a hand, and five-petalled flowers which are usually very showy. The shrubs described below flower all year round and are suitable for growing in the home while still small. Propagate by cuttings from late spring to late summer with bottom heat.* Hibiscus *is the Greek name for mallow, applied by Linnaeus to this closely related genus.*

Species cultivated

H. rosa-sinensis Rose of China Tropical Asia
An evergreen shrub growing to 2m (6½ft) or so in a pot. Leaves grow to 15cm (6in) long, oval, are often coarsely toothed and glossy green. Flowers are 10–15cm (4–6in) across, often more in selected cultivars, red in the type species, pink, apricot, orange, yellow and white in the many named cultivars grown chiefly in tropical and sub-tropical regions.

H.r. cooperi
Narrower leaves variegated with pink and white.

(illustrated overleaf)

31

KALANCHOE
Crassulaceae

Above *Hibiscus rosa-sinensis*

Origin: *Africa and southern Asia, one species in tropical America. A genus of 125 to 200 species of succulent shrubs and perennials some of which have been included in* Bryophyllum *and* Kitchingia. *They have fleshy leaves in opposite pairs and four-petalled tubular flowers which occur in panicles at the ends of the stems. They are good house and conservatory plants. Propagate by stem or leaf cuttings from late spring to summer or by seed in warmth in spring. Some species produce plantlets along the leaf edges and these can be detached and potted.* Kalanchoe *is a Latinized form of the Chinese name for one species.*

Species cultivated
K. blossfeldiana Flaming Katy Malagasy
Well-branched perennial growing to 30cm (1ft) tall. Leaves are 7cm

(2¾in) long, oval to oblong, rich shining green with a narrow red edge. Flowers are 1cm (⅜in) long, scarlet, borne in dense clusters from winter to early summer. A number of cultivars of this species have been raised with flowers in shades of red, orange and yellow. These are all good houseplants, but are short-day plants and normally flower only from late autumn to spring. By giving them extra darkness in summer (thereby reducing the daylight to 12 hours or less) they can be kept in flower all the year.

K. flammea Somali Republic

This is an erect perennial with sparingly branched stems growing to about 40cm (16in) or more tall. The leaves are oval, curved and toothed or smooth-edged, light grey-green, to 8cm (3in) long. Flowers are about 2cm (¾in) wide, orange-red or pink in colour, with a yellow tube, carried in corymbose clusters during the winter and spring.

Kalanchoe flammea

LACHENALIA
Liliaceae

Origin: *South Africa. A genus of 50 species of bulbous perennials, each bulb usually with two strap-shaped leaves, occasionally one or more than two. The cylindrical to bell-shaped flowers are carried in spikes above the foliage on leafless stalks. Propagate by offsets removed at potting time, or by seed in spring. The bulbs need a dry rest once the leaves begin to yellow. Lachenalia was named for Werner de la Chenal (1736–1800), who was Professor of Botany at Basle in Switzerland.*

Below Lachenalia aloides
Bottom Lachenalia reflexa

Species cultivated

L. aloides (*L. tricolor*) Cape cowslip Cape
Leaves grow to 2–2.5cm (¾–1in) wide, lance- to strap-shaped, dull green often with reddish-brown spotting. Flowers are 2.5cm (1in) long, yellow to greenish-yellow, orange-red at the base, the inner tepals edged with red-purple; they are hanging and carried on 15–30cm (6–12in) long stems. *L.a.* 'Aurea' is a soft orange-yellow without markings; 'Nelsonii' has longer, looser racemes of bright yellow flowers which are tipped with green; 'Quadricolor' has red and yellow flowers, the outer tepals edged with green, the inner with dark red.

L. bulbifera (*L. pendula*)
Leaves grow to 5cm (2in) wide, narrowly lance-shaped, dull green with no spotting. Flowers are 3–4cm (1¼–1½in) long, coral- to vermilion-red, sometimes tipped purplish-red and with a green marking at the apex, inner paler; they are borne on 15–25cm (6–10in) stems from late winter to spring. Forms with yellow colouring may be of hybrid origin.

L. × 'Pearsonii'

Vigorous hybrid, probably of *L. bulbifera*, with bright orange flowers edged with deep red and carried on stems to 45cm (1½ft) tall.

L. pendula See *L. bulbifera*.

L. reflexa

Two leaves per bulb, strap- to lance-shaped, up to 15cm (6in) in length, bright green, spreading to arching. Flowering stems are shorter than leaves, with a raceme of a few erect flowers at the end; each bloom about 2.5cm (1in) long, green-tinted yellow, borne in late winter to early spring.

L. tricolor See *L. aloides*.

LANTANA
Verbenaceae

Origin: *Tropical parts of the Americas and West Africa. A genus of 150 evergreen shrubs and perennials, those cultivated having opposite pairs of oval to oblong, toothed leaves and small, tubular, five-lobed flowers in dense, rounded, flattened heads. They make fine pot and tub plants for the conservatory and home. Propagate by cuttings in late summer, or in early spring in warmth.* Lantana *derives from an old Latin name for* Viburnum, *an unrelated genus with somewhat similar flowers.*

Species cultivated

L. camara Yellow sage Tropical America

Shrub growing to 1–2m (3–6½ft) tall, the stems sometimes prickly. Leaves are 5–10cm (2–4in) long, oval to oblong, dark green with a wrinkled appearance reminiscent of a sage leaf. Flowers grow in heads up to 5cm (2in) wide, the central florets opening yellow and ageing red or white, opening from late spring to autumn. Many forms and cultivars are grown with colours ranging from yellow to red, pink and white, but changing colour as they age; those listed as *L.c. hybrida* are shorter.

Lantana camara

LAPEIROUSIA (LAPEYROUSIA)
Iridaceae

Origin: *Temperate areas of South Africa. A genus of about 50 species of cormous plants. The narrow, sword-shaped leaves are borne in two ranks and the branched flower spikes carry six-petalled flowers usually in shades of pink or red. They flower from the summer onwards and can be stored dry in their pots over winter, then re-potted and brought into growth in early spring. They are very attractive flowering pot plants for the conservatory and can be brought into the house when they are ready to flower. Propagate by separating corms, or by seed in spring.*

Lapeirousia *was named for Baron Philippe Picot de la Peyrouse (1744–1818), a Pyrenean botanist.*

Lapeirousia laxa

Species cultivated
L. laxa (*L. cruenta, Anomatheca cruenta*)
Leaves are narrowly sword-shaped, growing to 20cm (8in) long, in fan-like tufts. Flowers grow up to 2.5cm (1in) long, slender-tubed, carmine-crimson, the outer three of the six spreading lobes bearing darker red blotches at the base; they are carried in short racemes on slender stems to 25cm (10in) tall. *L.l.* 'Alba' has pure white flowers.

LITHOPS
Aizoaceae
Living stones

Origin: *Southern Africa. A genus of about 50 species of solitary or clump-forming succulents, each stem made up of two very fleshy swollen leaves which are fused to form a reverse conical-shaped plant body, slit at the rounded or flattened top. Through the slit emerge in autumn the large, many-petalled, daisy-like flowers, which often completely hide the plant body beneath them. They should be treated as if cacti. There are many species available and those below are only a small selection of these. Propagate by separating individual plant bodies in the summer and treating as for cuttings, or by seed in spring.*

Lithops *derives from the Greek* lithos, *stone and* ops, *like.*

Lithops pseudotruncatella

Species cultivated
L. lesliei Transvaal, Cape
Solitary or forming small clumps, the plant bodies 3–4.5cm (1¼–1¾in) tall, with flattened tops, light brown or reddish-brown in colour, marked with dark greenish-brown spots and pits. The flowers are golden-yellow.

L. pseudotruncatella Namibia

Clump-forming, the plant bodies grow to 3cm (1¼in) high, very broadly reverse conical-shaped with a prominent fissure across the wide, flattish tops, light brownish-grey bearing a reddish-brown pattern of lines and dots. Flowers up to 3.5cm (1½in) wide, rich yellow. This is a variable species in the patterning and colouring of the plant bodies.

LOBIVIA
Cactaceae

Origin: *Andean South America. A genus of about 70 species of small to medium-sized rounded to short and cylindrical-shaped cacti. They have funnel- to bell-shaped flowers which are relatively large and usually colourful, opening by day and closing at night. They make attractive pot or pan plants. Propagate by seed or offsets.*

Lobivia *is an anagram of Bolivia, where many species are found growing wild.*

Species cultivated

L. pentlandii (*Echinopsis pentlandii*) Bolivia, Peru

Stems globular to short and cylindrical-shaped, up to 5–10cm (2–4in) tall, clump-forming, dark to greyish-green. Ten to 15 prominent ribs divided into large, oblong tubercles. Seven to 12 (sometimes as few as five) radial spines, brown, to 3cm (1¼in) long; plus one longer, straight or upwardly curved central spine. Flowers are funnel-shaped, up to 5–6cm (2–2½in) long and almost as wide, carmine-pink to orange-red. Fruit is globular, to 2cm (¾in) wide, green, edible and sweet. Several varieties are known, varying in stem shape and size and flower colour.

Lobivia pentlandii

Lotus mascaensis

LOTUS
Leguminosae

Origin: *Africa, Europe, Asia and North America, particularly in the Mediterranean region. A genus of about 100 species of perennials and sub-shrubs with trifoliate or pinnate leaves and typical pea flowers with strongly beaked keels, borne in axillary umbels. The species described are good pot plants for the conservatory or sunny window and are particularly decorative in a hanging basket. Propagate by seed in spring, or by cuttings in late summer. Lotus is from the Greek vernacular name* lotos *and is applied to various members of the pea family.*

Species cultivated

L. berthelotii Coral gem, Parrot's beak, Winged pea Canary Isles (Tenerife), Cape Verde Is.

Silvery-hairy sub-shrub with arching or trailing stems growing to 90cm (3ft) long. Leaves pinnate, made up of three to seven very narrow leaflets up to 1–2cm (⅜–¾in) long. Flowers up to 3cm (1¼in) long, scarlet to crimson, with a long-beaked keel and hood-shaped standard; they occur singly or in umbels of two to three or more in summer.

L. mascaensis Canary Isles (Tenerife)

Silvery-hairy shrub growing to 30cm (1ft) tall, spreading more widely. Pinnate leaves, with three to seven very narrow leaflets 1.2–1.5cm (½–⅝in) long. Flowers are 1.5–2cm (⅝–¾in) long, golden-yellow, the hooded standard flushed with red at the tip; they are borne in three- to seven-flowered clusters at the ends of the umbel in late spring and early summer.

MAMMILLARIA
Cactaceae

Origin: *S.W. North America to northern South America, but most in Mexico. A genus of 200 to 300 species of mostly small cacti with solitary or clustered, rounded to shortly cylindrical stems. They do not have ribs but are covered with prominent tubercles, sometimes spiralling around the plant. The areoles are woolly and the small funnel- or bell-shaped flowers are often freely borne from late spring and through summer. They are followed by club-shaped, usually pink or red fruits. Many are excellent pot or pan plants for the conservatory or windowsill and a great number are now commercially available. The species here are easy to grow and free-flowering. Propagate by offsets in summer or by seed in late spring.* Mammillaria *derives from the Latin* mammilla, *a teat, referring to the tubercles.*

Species cultivated

M. bombycina Northern Mexico

Stems clustering or sometimes solitary, globose at first then becoming shortly cylindrical, to 20cm (8in) in height. Tubercles in spirals, cylindrical, their axils woolly. Radial spines 30 to 40, white, pectinate, to 1cm (⅖in) long; centrals longer, dark tipped, the lower one hooked. Flowers are 1cm (⅜in) long, red.

M. multiceps (*M. prolifera multiceps*) Southern Texas, northern Mexico

Hummock-forming, reaching 15cm (6in) or more across; stems are shortly cylindrical, growing to 6cm (2½in) long, branching, covered with conical tubercles. White, numerous, hair-like radial spines, thicker central spines inclined, red-tipped when young. Flowers are yellow to whitish-yellow, funnel-shaped, and grow to 1.5cm (⅝in) long. Fruits are 1.2cm (½in) in length, bright rich red, edible.

Below *Mammillaria bombycina*
Below right *Mammillaria multiceps*

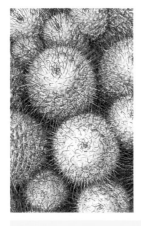

NOTOCACTUS

Cactaceae
Ball cacti

Origin: *Southern South America. A genus of 15 to 25 species of small, solitary or clustered cacti formerly included in the allied genus* Echinocactus. *They usually have prominent ribs with tubercles divided by deep notches and often densely felted areoles. The flowers are shortly funnel- to bell-shaped and are carried at the top of the plant body. Propagate clustered species by removing offsets; and all species by seed in spring.* Notocactus *comes from the Greek* noto, *southern and* cactus.

Notocactus scopa

Species cultivated

N. scopa S. Brazil, Uruguay
Stem like a globe, later becoming cylindrical, remaining solitary. Thirty to 35 notched ribs, the areoles with up to 40 white, bristle-like spines growing to 5mm (⅕in) long; four central spines, longer and thicker, brown. The flowers are up to 4cm (1½in) long.

OPUNTIA

Cactaceae
Prickly pears

Origin: *North and South America. A genus of 250 to 300 species of usually branched and shrubby cacti with distinctive jointed stems, the cylindrical or flattened sections known as pads. They have small, cylindrical or conical leaves which do not last for long, and abundant glochids and spines from the areoles. The short-tubed flowers have spreading petals which are often colourful and are followed by fleshy, frequently edible fruits. Prickly pears are suitable for both the conservatory and home when small and are easily propagated by seed in spring or by cuttings of mature pads in summer. This makes it a very simple job to replace a specimen which has outgrown its space.*

Opuntia *was originally named for a Greek plant that is now unidentifiable, and is used for this species for no obvious reason.*

Opuntia microdasys 'Albispina'

Species cultivated

O. microdasys (*O. pulvinata*) Bunny ears northern Mexico
Shrubby, growing to 90cm (3ft) tall. Oval pads, 8–15cm (3–6in), are finely downy. Areoles with a dense boss of golden glochids, sometimes with a single spine, often without. Flowers are 4–5cm (1½–2in) wide, yellow, followed by red, rounded fruit. *O.m.* 'Albispina' has smaller pads with silvery-white glochids.

OXALIS
Oxalidaceae
Wood sorrels

Oxalis deppei

Origin: *Cosmopolitan. A genus of about 850 species of annuals, perennials and shrubs some of which are bulbous or tuberous-rooted, some succulent. The leaves frequently have three leaflets, sometimes more, which fold up at night. Their flowers are five-petalled. When the fruits ripen seeds are ejected from their arils with force. The plants are suitable for a conservatory or sunny windowsill in the home. Propagate by division when planting, by seed in spring or by cuttings of the succulent species in summer. Oxalis derives from the Greek* oxys, *acid or sour, referring to the taste of the leaves.*

Species cultivated

O. deppei Lucky clover Mexico
Bulbous perennial with edible tubers which can reach 30cm (1ft) tall. Leaves with four broadly oval leaflets up to 4cm (1½in) long. Flowers grow to 2cm (¾in) long, red to rich purple, carried in umbels of five to 12 in summer. There is a white-flowered form.

PACHYPHYTUM
Crassulaceae
Moonstones

Origin: *Mexico. A genus of 12 species of succulents allied to Echeveria. They have very thick leaves usually in attractive shades of grey to blue-green and somewhat bell-like five-petalled flowers in*

Pachyphytum oviferum

cymes above the leaves. Propagate by stem and leaf cuttings or seed in late spring or summer. The species described here makes a welcome addition to a collection of succulents. Pachyphytum *derives from the Greek* pachys, *thick and* phyton, *a plant; the leaves are distended with water storage tissue.*

Species cultivated

P. oviferum Moonstones, Sugar almond plant
Stems eventually reach 10cm (4in) in length, sparingly branched, erect when young then prostrate or decumbent. The egg-shaped leaves are crowded at the stem tips, 2–4cm (¾–1½in) long, oval in cross-section, usually with a blue-white patina, sometimes lavender-tinted or reddish. Flowers are about 1.2cm (½in) long, rich red, and occur in cymes 5–13cm (2–5in) tall in late winter and spring.

PELARGONIUM

Geraniaceae
Geraniums

Origin: *Widespread throughout warm temperate areas of the New World, concentrated in South Africa but also in north Africa and the adjacent Atlantic islands and eastwards to Arabia and southern India, also in Australasia; those listed below are all from South Africa. Long ago included in* Geranium *and still often sold under that name. A genus of 250 to 280 species mainly of shrubs and sub-shrubs, but including annuals and perennials, most of which are adapted to areas of low rainfall. Some are succulent or almost so. Their main characteristics are the five-petalled flowers, which have a small nectary spur joined to the pedicel, and are carried in stalked, axillary umbels. The beaked fruit split open explosively when ripe into five sections each carrying with it a narrow segment of the style. The species described below are all good house and conservatory plants, flowering in summer. Propagate by seed in spring or by cuttings taken in spring or summer.* Pelargonium *is derived from the Greek* pelargos, *a stork, an allusion to the long-beaked fruit.*

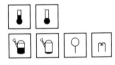

Pelargonium betulinum

Species cultivated

P. betulinum
Shrubby, fairly erect and slender, eventually growing to 90cm (3ft) in height. Leaves are broadly oval, toothed, 1–2cm (⅜–¾in) long, leathery-textured and tinted blue-green. Flowers are 2–2.5cm (¾–1in) wide, white or pink with a carmine vein pattern at the base of the two upper petals, usually occurring in two- or three-bloomed umbels.
P. × domesticum Regal/Fancy/Show geraniums (in US Martha/Lady Washington geraniums)
Hybrid group involving *P. angulosum, P. cucullatum, P. fulgidum, P.*

41

Above Pelargonium ×
domesticum 'Rembrandt'
Above right Pelargonium ×
hortorum 'Mr Henry Cox'

Pelargonium peltatum

grandiflorum and other species. They are mostly compact, shrubby, 40–60cm (16–24in) tall or more. Leaves are 5–10cm (2–4in) wide, usually shallowly lobed, sometimes more deeply so, with toothed edges. Flowers are 4–5cm (1½–2in) wide in shades of white, pink, red and purple, blotched with darker shades.

P. × hortorum Zonal geraniums

Complex hybrid group involving *P. inquinans, P. zonale* and other species. They are shrubby, and grow to 1.5m (5ft) or more tall. Leaves are 6–13cm (2½–5in) across, rounded to kidney-shaped, with scalloped and waved edges, usually mid-green with a darker brown or bronze, horseshoe-shaped mark in the centre. Flowers are 2–5cm (¾–2in) wide, in shades of red, pink, orange, white and purple, some bicoloured and some with different-coloured edges; they can be single or double and may have quilled petals. Cultivars with variegated leaves are also grown, the markings varying from white and yellow to crimson or brown, and some have dark green or purplish foliage.

P. peltatum Ivy-leaved geranium

Stems grow to 1m (3ft) or more long, and are slender and trailing. Leaves are 5–7cm (2–2¾in) wide, somewhat fleshy, five-angled or lobed, rather ivy-like but peltate, the leaf stalk joining the leaf a little way in from the edge. Flowers are 3–4cm (1¼–1½in) wide, pink to carmine, with darker markings on the upper petals. Some of the named forms available are probably of hybrid origin.

P. violareum (*P. tricolor, P. splendidum violareum*)

Shrubby, well-branched species, spreading to 45cm (1½ft) or so by 30cm (1ft) in height. Leaves are usually oval, sometimes lance-shaped, irregularly toothed, and occasionally have a few narrow lobes. They are grey and covered with short, soft hairs, usually growing to about 4cm (1½in) long. Flowers are about 2.5cm (1in) wide, composed of five rounded petals, the upper two red to red-purple, darker at their

Pelargonium violareum

bases, the lower ones white or palest pink; the flowering stems branch, carrying two or more umbels each with two to six blooms, mainly in spring and summer.

PENTAS

Rubiaceae

Origin: *Africa, Arabia and Malagasy. A genus of 35 to 50 species of shrubs or perennials having hairy, opposite, smooth-edged leaves and clusters of small, long, tubular flowers with five spreading lobes. The species described below makes an excellent pot plant. Cut back plants in late winter after flowering and either take the young shoots as cuttings in spring, or, if a large plant is required, pot-on the original plant.* Pentas *derives from the Greek* pentos, *five, the genus differing from most members of the* Rubiaceae *family in having its floral parts in fives.*

Species cultivated
P. lanceolata (*P. carnea*) (Egyptian) Star cluster Tropical East Africa to southern Arabia

Pentas lanceolata

Sub-shrub, growing 90cm (3ft) or more tall though flowering at 30–60cm (1–2ft) in a pot. Leaves are 4–9cm (1½–3½in) long, lance- to oval, hairy, and carried in opposite pairs. Flowers are 2–4cm (¾–1½in) long, white, pink, red, lilac or magenta, in showy corymbs at the ends of the stems in late summer and autumn.

PLEIOSPILOS
Aizoaceae

Pleiospilos nellii

Origin: *South Africa. A genus of about 35 species of virtually stemless succulents, some of which look like stones in the same way as* Lithops. *They may be clump-forming or solitary, each very short stem bearing two to four, sometimes more, pairs of very thick fleshy leaves. The daisy-like flowers are unusually large for the size of the plant and showy. The species described here is a desirable addition to a collection of succulents.* Pleiospilos *derives from the Greek* pleios, *many and* spilos, *a speck or spot; most, if not all, of the species have conspicuously dotted leaves.*

Species cultivated
P. nellii Cape

With two pairs of small, nearly hemispherical leaves and flowers of a pale salmon-orange with a white centre.

PLUMBAGO
Plumbaginaceae
Leadworts

Origin: *Widespread in the warmer regions of the world. A genus of 12 to 20 species of shrubs, sub-shrubs, perennials and annuals, with alternate, smooth-edged leaves and slender tubular flowers opening to five broad lobes and carried in spikes or panicles at the ends of the stems. They are good container plants, flowering when small.* P. auriculata *needs support for its partially climbing stems and responds*

Plumbago auriculata

to hard pruning in late winter, having its side branches cut back to within a few centimetres of the main stem. Propagate by cuttings of non-flowering shoots in warmth in summer, also by seed in spring. Plumbago derives from the Latin plumbum, *lead, one species having the reputation to cure lead poisoning.*

Species cultivated

P. auriculata (*P. capensis*) Blue Cape plumbago/leadwort South Africa

Straggling, climbing or scrambling shrub, easily kept to 3m (10ft) in a pot, but growing to 6m (20ft) in the open, its slender stems needing support and best treated as for a climber. Leaves are 5cm (2in) long, oval to oblong, spatula-like, and evergreen. Flowers grow to 4cm (1½in) long, are sky-blue and open from summer to autumn. *P.a.* 'Alba' has white flowers. Best grown in temperate conditions, but will survive cooler temperatures.

PORTULACA
Portulaceae

Origin: *Tropics and warm temperate regions, particularly the Americas. A genus of 100 to 200 species, depending upon the classification followed, of annuals and perennials. Their leaves are alternate, or almost opposite, oval to very narrow and often fleshy. The flowers open their five spreading petals only in sun. The species described is a colourful annual for a pot. Propagate by seed in spring.* Portulaca *is from the Latin vernacular name for purslane.*

Portulaca grandiflora

Species cultivated

P. grandiflora Sun plant Brazil, Uruguay, Argentina

Tufted annual growing to 15cm (6in) or more in height with spreading to ascending stems. Leaves are 2.5cm (1in) long, cylindrical and fleshy. Flowers are 2–3cm (¾–1¼in) across, open wide in sun, and occur in a range of colours including reds, pinks, yellows, purples and white, both single and double forms being grown; they have a central boss of bright yellow stamens and each flower sits above a leafy collar.

PROSTANTHERA
Labiatae
Mint bushes

Origin: *Australia. A genus of 50 species of aromatic, evergreen shrubs with opposite, toothed leaves and tubular two-lipped flowers, the upper lip made up of two lobes, the lower made up of three. They are*

carried in leafy racemes or panicles in spring and summer. The species described makes an attractive pot or tub plant and can be brought into the home for flowering. Propagate by seed in spring in warmth, or by cuttings in summer with bottom heat. Prostanthera is derived from the Greek prosthema, an appendage and the Latin anthera, an anther, because of the spur-like outgrowths on the anthers.

Species cultivated
P. melissifolia Balm mint bush Victoria
Slender shrub growing up to 1–3m (3–10ft) tall, flowering when small. Leaves are 2–5cm (¾–2in) long, oval, coarsely toothed and strongly aromatic. Flowers are 1.5cm (⅝in) long, lavender to purple, wreathing the stems in spring and early summer.

Prostanthera melissifolia

REBUTIA
Cactaceae

Origin: *Bolivia and Argentina. A genus of 27 species of small cacti with globular or somewhat elongated, solitary or clustered stems. They have prominent areoles and freely borne colourful flowers opening around the base of the stem in late spring, making good pot plants for the home or conservatory. Propagate by seed in spring or by offsets in summer.* Rebutia *was named for Mons. P. Rebut, a French cactus dealer at the end of the nineteenth century.*

Species cultivated
R. minuscula Red crown cactus, Mexican sunball N.W. Argentina
Single or clustering stems are globular, somewhat flattened and sunken at the top, 4–5cm (1½–2in) thick; tubercles in about 20 spiralling rows are pale green. About 30 white, radial spines are 3–6mm (⅛–¼in) long. Crimson flowers grow to 4cm (1½in) long.

Rebutia violaciflora

R. senilis Fire crown cactus Argentina
Stems are globular, growing to 7cm (2¾in) tall and wide, and are clump-forming and pale green; the tubercles are spiralling. Twenty-five to 40 glassy-white tipped brown spines up to 1.3cm (½in) long. Flowers up to 5cm (2in) long are carmine-red.

R. violaciflora Argentina
Stems globular, growing to 4–5cm (1½–2in) tall and clustering; tubercles spiralling, in 20 to 25 rows. Fifteen to 25 white to yellowish, radial spines, reach 5–10mm (³⁄₁₆–³⁄₈in) long. Flowers grow to 4cm (1½in) long and are magenta-red.

RHODOHYPOXIS
Hypoxidaceae

Origin: *South Africa. A genus of two species of small, rhizomatous perennials, which make colourful plants for the conservatory or home when flowering. Propagate by separating the rhizomes (the only method for named cultivars) or by seed sown in spring. Plants raised from seed often show shades of pink, light red and white.* Rhodo-hypoxis *derives from the Greek* rhodo, *red and the genus* Hypoxis.

Rhodohypoxis baurii

Species cultivated
R. baurii South Africa
Clump-forming perennial with egg-shaped, corm-like rhizomes. Leaves, which reach 5cm (2in) or more in length, all rise from the base of the plant, and are very narrow, pointed and with white hairs. Flowers are 2cm (¾in) wide, pink to red, and grow one to a stem on stems equalling or shorter than the leaves; they open from summer to autumn. 'Allbrighton Red' is deep red; 'Fred Broome' is a creamy pink; 'Margaret Rose' is a bright pink; *R.b. platypetala* has white or pink-tinted flowers.

ROSMARINUS
Labiatae

Origin: *Mediterranean region. A genus of three species of evergreen, aromatic shrubs having opposite pairs of leaves with rolled edges. The two-lipped flowers are in shades of blue. They make attractive pot plants for the conservatory or home, adding a bonus of leaves for cooking. Propagate by cuttings in late summer in cool conditions.*

Species cultivated
R. officinalis Rosemary
An erect or semi-erect shrub, which rarely grows over 1m (3ft) in a pot, but more than this in the open garden. Leaves are 2–5cm (¾–2in)

Rosmarinus officinalis

long, dark green above, with close white hairs beneath. Flowers, which grow to 2cm (¾in) long, are blue to lavender-blue, in clusters of two or three from the leaf axils in spring and summer, sometimes in the autumn also. 'Albiflorus' has white flowers; 'Benenden Blue' is shorter with brighter blue flowers; 'Fastigiatus' ('Miss Jessop's Upright') has erect stems and strong growth; 'Roseus' has lilac-pink flowers; and 'Severn Sea' is dwarf with arching branches and bright blue flowers. Hardy.

RUSSELIA
Scrophulariaceae

Origin: *Mexico to tropical South America. Depending upon the botanical authority, a genus of 20 to 50 species of shrubs and sub-shrubs, a few of which provide the conservatory with some highly decorative pot plants. Their stems may be erect, semi-climbing or hanging, in some species green and rush-like with small scale-like leaves that soon fall. The flowers are tubular to funnel-shaped and slightly two-lipped, usually produced in abundance. Propagate by cuttings or layering in spring or summer, or by division in spring. Russelia honours Dr Alexander Russell (c. 1715–68), resident doctor to the English Factory at Aleppo and a keen natural historian.*

Species cultivated
R. equisetiformis (*R. juncea*) Coral plant Fountain bush Mexico, naturalized widely elsewhere in the tropics and sub-tropics.

Russelia equisetiformis

Shrub with many branches, which grows to 90cm (3ft) or more in height; four-angled, rush-like, bright green stems in mature plants are hanging. Flowers are tubular, 2.5cm (1in) long, bright red, and borne in summer.

SANDERSONIA

Liliaceae

Origin: *South Africa. A genus of one species of tuberous-rooted perennial which makes a distinctive pot plant. Propagate by seed in spring or by separating the tubers when re-potting; it will flower in two to three years from seed. Sandersonia was named for John Sanderson (1820–81), secretary of the Horticultural Society of Natal and the discoverer of this plant.*

Sandersonia aurantiaca

Species cultivated

S. aurantiaca South Africa

Stems are erect, reclining or partially climbing and 30–60cm (1–2ft) tall. Leaves grow to 10cm (4in) long and are alternate, very narrow to lance-shaped with ends which sometimes terminate in hooks. Flowers are 2.5cm (1in) long, the six tepals joined, almost globe-shaped, dividing to six very shallow lobes at the constricted mouth, the whole very reminiscent of a nodding Chinese lantern: they are orange in colour and carried on slender stalks.

SAUROMATUM

Araceae

Origin: *Tropical Africa and Asia to western Malaysia. A genus of four to six species of tuberous-rooted perennials, each with a one-stalked*

Sauromatum guttatum

leaf and an arum-like spadix within a spathe. The species described below is the only one generally available and can be flowered without soil, but after this treatment they are usually discarded. If, however, they are potted in the normal way in a good compost, the tuber will produce its attractive leaf after the flowers have died down. Once the leaf yellows, dry off the tuber until early spring, when it will start new growth. The plant is worth growing for its leaves alone. When blooming it gives off a strong smell of bad meat and is best put out of the living area for a few days. Propagate by separating offsets. Sauromatum *derives from the Greek* sauros, *a lizard, referring to the mottled appearance of the inside of the spathe.*

Species cultivated
S. guttatum Voodoo lily, Monarch of the East India
The rounded, flattened tuber can reach 6–13cm (2½–5in) across; it produces a single leaf 60–90cm (2–3ft) long of which two-thirds or so is stalk. The leaf blade is divided into three lobes, the side ones again divided into lance-shaped to oblong lobes. Flowers are small and petalless, borne at the base of a stiff, tail-like, deep purple spadix, which remains erect for only a matter of hours, then starts to bend. The spathe is shorter than the spadix, being about 30cm (1ft) long, and is greenish on the back and yellowish inside with deep purple spotting and blotching.

SCHINUS
Anacardiaceae

Origin: *Mexico to Argentina and Chile. A genus of about 30 species of evergreen, single sex shrubs and trees, a few of which are widely grown in warm temperate and tropical regions and for their leaves under glass. The species described here makes a good tub specimen for the conservatory or large room. It has undivided or pinnately compound, alternate leaves and panicles of tiny five-petalled flowers. It produces berry-like fruits. Propagate by seed in spring or by cuttings in summer.* Schinus *derives from the Greek name* schinos *used for the mastic tree (*Pistacia lentiscus*); some species yield a similar gum or resin.*

Species cultivated
S. molle Peruvian pepper/mastic tree Peru (Andes region)
A small to medium-sized tree with hanging branchlets, twigs and leaves, which is easily kept to about 2m (6½ft) in a container. Leaves are 10–22cm (4–9in) long, pinnate, and composed of 15 to 41 narrowly lance-shaped, rich green leaflets. Flowers are a whitish colour. Fruits are like tiny rose-red peas, but only occur if a plant of each sex is present.

Schinus molle

SENECIO

Compositae

Origin: *Cosmopolitan. A genus of between 2,000 and 3,000 species of annuals, perennials, climbers, trees and shrubs, including some succulents – the largest genus of flowering plants. All species have alternate leaves and daisy-like flowers, sometimes without ray florets, most frequently in clusters that occur at the ends of the stems. They require only light watering. Propagate all species by seed; the succulents by cuttings in summer. Senecio derives from the Latin* senex, *an old man, referring to the white-hairy pappus of some species.*

Species cultivated

S. articulatus (*Kleinia articulatus*) Candle plant South Africa
Succulent shrub growing up to 30–60cm (1–2ft) tall. Stems are 1.5–2cm (⅝–¾in) across, cylindrical, and divided with marked joints, grey-green. Leaves grow to 5cm (2in) long, are deeply three- to five-lobed, short-lived, appearing briefly in the winter on young stems only. Flower heads are about 1.5cm (⅝in) long, yellowish-white, rather like those of groundsel. Propagate by stem sections, which can be removed, or they sometimes fall off, at the joints.

S. haworthii (*Kleinia haworthii, K. tomentosa*) South Africa
Erect, sparingly branched, succulent shrub growing to 30cm (1ft) in height, the fairly robust stems densely white-felted. Leaves are more or less erect, 2–4cm (¾–1½in) or more long, tapering to each end, and also densely white-felted. Flower heads are groundsel-like, orange, usually occurring one to each long stalk.

S. rowleyanus String of beads S.W. Africa
Succulent perennial with slender, prostrate or hanging stems 60–90cm (2–3ft) long. Leaves are 5–12mm (⅕–⅜in) across, almost

Senecio haworthii

spherical, bright green with a translucent band around one side and a small sharp point. Flower heads are 1.5–2cm (⅝–¾in) long and made up of long white disc florets with purple stamen tubes, giving the effect of tiny shaving brushes. Very good in a hanging basket. Grows well if kept warm, but flowers best after a cool spell in early winter.

SETCREASEA

Commelinaceae

Setcreasea pallida
'Purple Heart'

Origin: Mexico to USA (Texas). A genus of six species of perennials allied to Tradescantia. *They are tufted to clump-forming, somewhat fleshy with alternate oval to oblong leaves and three petalled flowers occurring within boat-shaped bracts. The species described below is a familiar house and conservatory plant. Repot annually in late spring and slightly shade from full summer sun. Propagate by division or by cuttings from spring to autumn.* Setcreasea *is a name of unknown derivation.*

Species cultivated

S. pallida Mexico
Erect to trailing plant with slender stems up to 40cm (16in) long. Leaves are 8–15cm (3–6in) long, oblong, fleshy. Flowers are about 2cm (¾in) across, mauve to lavender-pink, clustered at the ends of the stems. 'Purple Heart' (*S. purpurea*, Purple heart) is a form with dark, violet-purple leaves and red-purple flowers.

SOLANUM

Solanaceae

Origin: Cosmopolitan. A genus of about 1,700 species of annuals, perennials, shrubs and climbers with alternate leaves. The flowers, which can be one to each stem or in clusters, look initially as if they are on lateral shoots, but on close examination it can be seen that they do not arise in the leaf axils. They do, in fact, grow from the ends of the stems, the growth being continued by an axillary stem which grows beyond the previous main stem. Flowers have the corolla fused at the base, opening to five spreading lobes, with a prominent central cone of yellow stamens. They are followed by rounded berries, poisonous in some species, edible in others. The climbers described below are best in a conservatory and, being vigorous, it is advisable to prune them every spring, the rest are suitable for growing in the house. Propagate shrubs and climbers by cuttings in summer or by seed in spring. S. capsicastrum *and* S. pseudocapsicum *are usually propagated annually, sowing seed in spring in warmth, pricking off and potting-on as soon as they are large enough, finally using up to*

13cm or 15cm (5in or 6in) pots. Solanum *is an old Latin name probably for* S. nigrum, *the black nightshade.*

Species cultivated

S. capsicastrum Winter cherry Brazil

Evergreen shrub reaching 60cm (2ft) or more, but usually grown as an annual and then rarely exceeding 30cm (1ft). Leaves are 4–7cm (1½–2¾in) long, oval to broadly lance-shaped with short, branching hairs, each large leaf with a small one at its base. Flowers, which are about 1cm (⅜in) wide, white, and carried singly or in pairs, are followed by egg-shaped, pointed, scarlet berries 1.5–2cm (⅝–¾in) long. Often confused with *S. pseudocapsicum*. For *S.c.* 'Nanum' see *S. pseudocapsicum* 'Nanum'.

S. crispum Chilean potato tree Chile

Scrambling, evergreen shrub growing to 4m (13ft). Leaves are 6–10cm (2½–4in) long, oval to lance-shaped, often waved (crisped). Flowers are 2cm (¾in) across, blue-purple and occur in dense clusters in summer and autumn, followed by small, rounded yellowish-white berries. A white form is known. *S.c.* 'Glasnevin' is free-flowering.

S. jasminoides Potato vine, Jasmine nightshade Brazil

Semi-twining, slender-stemmed climber growing to 5m (16ft). Leaves are 3–7cm (1¼–2¾in) long, smooth-edged or with irregular-pinnate lobes. Flowers grow to 2.5cm (1in) across with broad lobes, pale blue to light mauve, in branched cymes in summer and autumn. *S.j.* 'Album' has pure white flowers.

S. pseudocapsicum Jerusalem cherry Eastern South America, but widely naturalized in the tropics and sub-tropics

Erect shrub growing 1m (3ft) or more tall. Leaves are 5–10cm (2–4in) long, oblong to lance-shaped, glossy green, hairless, in pairs often of unequal size. Flowers are 1.5cm (⅝in) across, white, occurring singly or in twos or threes, followed by globe-shaped berries 1–1.5cm (⅜–⅝in) across, red, poisonous. Distinguished from *S. capsicastrum* (with which it is much confused) by its smaller, round berries and smooth leaves. 'Nanum' is dwarf, compact and bushy; 'Patersonii' is dwarf but of a spreading habit.

Solanum crispum

SPREKELIA

Amaryllidaceae

Origin: *Mexico. This is a genus of only one species – a handsome, bulbous plant that is suitable for growing in the conservatory or home. Pot in late winter or early spring leaving the neck of the bulb above soil level. Dry off as the leaves yellow in autumn and keep dry at about 7–10°C (45–50°F) until late winter. Propagate by offsets or seed.* Sprekelia *was named for Johann Heinrich von Sprekelsen*

Sprekelia formosissima   *(1691–1764), a German lawyer who was also a very keen amateur botanist and gardener.*

Species cultivated

S. formosissima (*Amaryllis formosissima*) Jacobean/Aztec lily
Leaves grow to 30cm (1ft) tall and are strap-shaped. Flowers reach 10cm (4in) long with six tepals; the upper one is broad and stands erect or curving back at the tip, those at the sides are narrower, curved and spreading, the bottom three overlapping to form a shape like the lip of an orchid; they are bright crimson and borne singly on 30cm (1ft) scapes in spring or summer as new leaves develop.

STRELITZIA

Strelitziaceae (Musaceae)
Bird of Paradise flower

Origin: *Sub-tropical to southern Africa. A genus of four to five species of evergreen perennials and small trees of palm-like form having long, undivided, leathery leaves usually in two ranks. The flowers are asymmetrical with three narrow sepals and three petals, two of which are joined to form a tongue-shaped structure. Several flowers are grouped together within a horizontally borne boat-shaped bract. Propagate by division or by seed sown in warmth, both in spring.* Strelitzia *was named for Charlotte of Mecklenberg-Strelitz (1744– 1818), who became the wife of George III of England.*

Species cultivated

S. reginae Bird of paradise flower South Africa
Clump-forming, growing to 1m (3ft) tall. Leaves are long-stalked, with blades 25–45cm (10–18in) long, oblong to lance-shaped, grey to blue-green, blue-green beneath, leathery in texture. Flowers with three orange or yellow sepals, one small orange petal and the joined pair blue, borne within a 15–20cm (6–8in) long, narrowly red-edged, boat-shaped bract in spring and summer. *S.r. juncea* has robust, rush-like leaf stalks usually without (but sometimes with very small) blades at the ends; *S.r. intermedia* is half-way between variety *juncea* and the type species, having much reduced leaf blades; and *S.r. humilis* is much dwarfer than the type.

Strelitzia reginae juncea

STREPTOSOLEN

Solanaceae

Streptosolen jamesonii

Origin: *Andean Colombia and Ecuador. A genus of one species of evergreen, semi-scrambling shrub with abundant colourful flowers. It is a good container plant for the conservatory, where it can be grown on the back wall, in free-standing pots or in hanging baskets. Cut back old stems by one-third in late winter to keep the plants bushy. Propagate by cuttings of young stems in late spring.* Streptosolen *derives from the Greek* streptos, *twisted and* solen, *a tube, from the twisted corolla tubes.*

Species cultivated

S. jamesonii Marmalade bush Colombia, Ecuador
Capable of reaching 1.8m (6ft), but easily kept smaller. Leaves are alternate, up to 3cm (1¼in) long, oval, deep green, with a finely wrinkled surface. Flowers are 3–4cm (1¼–1½in) long, the twisted tube opening to a widely flared, five-lobed mouth; they are bright orange with a paler tube and carried in panicles 10–20cm (4–8in) long at the ends of the stems from late spring to late summer.

TIBOUCHINA

Melastomataceae

Origin: *Central and South America. A genus of about 350 species of shrubs, sub-shrubs, climbers and perennials, with opposite, undivided leaves and usually showy flowers with five (occasionally four) petals and sepals. The species described makes an attractive pot or tub plant. To keep plants small, cut back their stems annually to 15cm (6in) in late winter or early spring. They can be trained to cover the back wall of a conservatory, but the lateral stems must be cut back to two pairs of buds in spring to prevent the plant from becoming too leggy. Propagate by cuttings in spring or summer with bottom heat.* Tibouchina *is a Latin form of the Guyanan common name.*

Species cultivated

T. urvilleana (*T. semidecandra*) Glory bush Brazil
Shrub growing to 3–5m (10–16ft) tall, but easily kept below half this; evergreen in tropical temperatures, when it will flower intermittently throughout the year; deciduous in cool conditions, then flowering in summer and autumn only. Stems are four-angled, finely covered with red hairs. Leaves are 7–15cm (2¾–6in) long, oval to oblong with three to seven sunken longitudinal veins, rich green, velvety hairy. Flowers are 7–10cm (2¾–4in) wide, satiny royal purple, with darker, curiously hooked stamens opening from rose-red buds.

Tibouchina urvilleana

TITANOPSIS

Aizoaceae

Origin: *South Africa. A genus of six to eight species of succulents which mimic the limestone rock of their homeland. They are hummock-forming when mature, made up of rosette-like shoots of opposite leaf pairs. Each leaf is spatula-shaped with an obliquely triangular tip thickly covered with white to grey-white low tubercles of irregular size. The autumn-borne flowers are large and showy. The species described here is easily grown.* Titanopsis *derives from* Titans, *in Greek*

Titanopsis calcarea

mythology the twelve children of Uranus and Gaea, of whom one, Hyperion, was sun god and opsis, *like; the mainly yellow flowers are likened to the sun.*

Species cultivated
T. calcarea Cape
Leaves are about 2.5cm (1in) long, the tips broadly and bluntly triangular, the grey-white tubercles sometimes with a faintly bluish tinge. Flowers are 2cm (¾in) wide, bright golden-yellow, sometimes almost orange.

TRACHYCARPUS
Palmae

Trachycarpus fortunei

Origin: *Himalaya to S.E. Asia. A genus of six to eight species of small- to medium-sized palms. They have fan-shaped leaves divided to more than half-way into very narrow segments. The plants are surprisingly frost-hardy and are suitable for a cold or cool conservatory or room. Propagate by seed in spring in the warm.* Trachycarpus *derives from the Greek* trachys, *rough and* karpos, *fruit.*

Species cultivated
T. fortunei Windmill/Chusan palm Borneo to East China
These grow to 2m (6½ft) or more in a container, to 10m (33ft) in the open. They have a single stem covered with brown fibrous leaf bases. Leaves grow to 60cm (2ft) long in a pot, but to twice this in the open, and are fan-shaped to almost rounded, divided deeply into many narrow, pleated segments. Young plants do not produce flowers.

TROPAEOLUM
Tropaeolaceae

Origin: *Mexico, Central and South America. A genus of 50 to 90 species, depending upon the classification followed. They are annual and perennial climbers, often with tuberous roots. The alternate leaves, which can be rounded to shield-shaped to compound, have stalks capable of twisting and acting as tendrils. The flowers have five sepals, the uppermost with a long nectary spur, and five broad petals. They are pot plants for the conservatory or home. Propagate the perennial kinds by seed when ripe, by offsets or division, or by cuttings of basal shoots removed close to the tuber in spring and rooted with bottom heat. Propagate annuals by seed sown in spring.* Tropaeolum *derives from the Latin* tropaeum, *a trophy, a plant of* T. majus *in flower on a support is said to resemble a trophy pillar hung with shields (leaves) and bloody helmets (flowers) of the defeated enemy!*